The Way to Salvation In the Light of Surah Al-Asr

By

Dr. Israr Ahmad

Translated by

Dr. Absar Ahmad & Dr. Sanaullah Ansari

دار الثقافة
Dar Ul Thaqafah

Dar Ul Thaqafah

Dar ul Thaqafah
www.darulthaqafah.com
https://twitter.com/darulthaqafah

Find our titles on your favorite online bookstore using the keyword 'Dar Ul Thaqafah'.

2023 CE – 1444 H

Translation of the Qur'ān

It should be perfectly clear that the Qur'ān is only authentic in its original language, Arabic. Since perfect translation of the Qur'ān is impossible, we have used the translation of the meaning of the Qur'ān throughout the book, as the result is only a crude meaning of the Arabic text.

Qur'ānic verses appear in speech marks proceeded by a reference to the Surah and verse number. Sayings (*Hadith*) of Prophet Muhammad (saw) appear in inverted commas along with reference to the Hadith Book and its Reporter.

Contents

In the name of Allah, Most Gracious, Most Merciful.

1. *By (the Token of) Time (through the Ages),*
2. *Verily Men are In a state of loss,*
3. *Except those who have Faith, And do righteous deeds, And join together In the mutual teaching Of Truth, and of Patience and Constancy.*

Foreword

This booklet includes two papers on the same topic. The first one was published in the monthly 'MEESAQ' Lahore in 1966. The second is a speech which was delivered before a gathering of the staff and senior students of Aitchison College, Lahore (Pakistan). The speech was taped by the Principal, and was transcribed later. It appeared in the monthly 'MEESAQ' of June, 1973. The Principal of Aitchison College also published it and distributed it freely. I pray that these sincere efforts of the former Principal of Aitchison College may be accepted by Allah, and may He shower His blessings on him in this world and in the Hereafter. Both the articles are now being published together by Markazi Anjuman Khuddamul Quran, Lahore.

As the topic of both articles is the same, naturally there might be some repetition. It might be asked what was the necessity of publishing both of them. In this connection it may be pointed out that the style and standard of both differ in many respects. The first one is a written document in which, leaving aside the mental horizon of readers, the thoughts have been expressed smoothly and fluently in a particular style of writing and in a special linguistic tone.

The second article is basically a speech and its style portrays the sense of the spoken discourse and the language used is comparatively simpler. In this way the combination of these two articles, it is hoped, has enhanced its utility and efficacy.

Secondly, when studied seriously, it would become clear that wherever something has been repeated, it has also brought out a new point and there are many important items, which are either in the first one and absent in the other and vice versa. Both these articles are based on the sole aim, that is: to explain to Muslims the correct doctrine of eternal salvation and deliverance, and the practical demands of the Islamic faith. For this objective, I have compiled a selected course of the Holy Quran, the starting point of which is *Surah Al-'Asr.* If Allah so wishes and gives us the means, we intend to bring out the entire course in the form of such booklets for our readers.

Dr Israr Ahmad

The Way To Salvation In The Light Of Surah Al-'Asr

SURAH AL-'ASR, *a* very early Makkan *surah* is one of the shortest *surahs* of the Quran. The words used in this *surah* are also commonly used in Urdu and are familiar to those who have a fair knowledge of this language. This is why a sketchy meaning of the *surah* is grasped without much difficulty by every Urdu-knowing individual. But studied and pondered over at a deeper level, this *Surah* opens up a treasure house of knowledge and wisdom.

As a matter of fact, there is a striking analogy between this *surah* and *Surah Al-Ikhlas. Surah Al- 'Asr* sums up in a few concise words the way and practical guidance that leads to eternal success and salvation just as *Surah Al-Ikhlas* delineates in a few words the nature and unity of Godhood in Islam. Though very short and compact, both of these *surahs* are extremely rich in meaning relating to their respective themes. On this ground Maulana Hamid-ud-Din Farahi has categorized *Surah Al- 'Asr* as an aphorism of great wisdom, whereas *lmam Al-Sha'feii* maintained that a deep and thoughtful study of this *surah* alone provides adequate guidance for attaining one's salvation.

This *surah* is composed of three verses. The second verse is of central importance in meaning and significance. This verse expresses the painful and tragic state of man generally, a state of loss and deprivation. The evidence for this is presented in the first verse, in the form of an oath or adjuration. The third verse of the *surah* carves out an exception from the general condition of man laid down in the second verse.

In this way, this *surah* is clearly divided into two parts. Its first part 'By fleeting time, verily man is doomed (or destined) to loss and ruin'—consists of a statement and its proof and as such is of immense philosophical significance, whereas the second part of the *surah* —'Save those who believe, and do righteous deeds, and unite for the sake of truth and steadfastness'— is of utmost practical importance, giving the essential requirements and conditions of a successful life, a precise but nevertheless complete and comprehensive elucidation of the 'right path'.

Big Impact

It is not my aim to write down, in the following pages, an exegetical explanation of this *surah,* firstly because this venture calls for greater scholarship and deeper insight than I can claim and, secondly, because in my opinion Maulana Hameed-ud-Din Farahi has already done full justice to the elucidation and exposition of the profound meaning of this *surah.* In the following discussion an attempt has been made merely at explaining some general principles of the *surah* and, in particular, some crucial points of its second part so that a detailed and synoptic view of the obligations and duties that Islam enjoins upon us is put in bold relief.

If we look at this *surah* as a whole, we realize that the note of warning and admonition is much more pronounced than the conditions for hope given at the end. Firstly, its very opening statement produces a big impact on the reader. The words 'By (the token of) time, verily man is in a state of loss even if considered only in their vocal effect, are capable of giving a big jolt and arousing the listener from his slumber. A full realization of its meaning must produce a still more potent effect.

Secondly; the statement, 'Verily man is doomed to failure', has been laid down as an all- compassing and categorical assertion. On the other hand, the verse starting with the words, 'except those who have faith. . .' grants an exception to the general statement. This is tantamount to saying that whereas the loss or doom of man is almost a universal truth, salvation is an exception to be achieved by only a few.

A statement very similar to this has been made in *Surah At-Teen* (XCV). The verse of this *surah,*

"Then we reduced him to the lowest of the low" describes the depraved condition of mankind as a whole, while the next part of this verse *'Save those who believe and do good deeds'* marks out the persons saved from the state of depravity.

But in *Surah At-Teen* two optimistic points have been made to lighten the note of warning. One, prior to, "Then we reduced him to the lowest of the low" a re-assurance of the primordial goodness of man has been given in these words:

"Surely we created man in the best of moulds". Two, immediately after the words "Save those who believe and do good deeds", a heart-warming promise of eternal salvation has been made in the same verse, 'and theirs is a reward unfailing'. In *Surah AI-'Asr,* on the contrary, not only there is no reassurance of man's creation 'in the best of moulds', but also it lacks a positive promise of an 'unfailing reward'. It ends with a mere statement of the possibility of deliverance from loss and ruin. Further, in *Surah At-Teen* only two conditions have been laid that exempt one from falling into a depraved state *i.e.,* belief and good deeds, *Surah Al-'Asr* demands for the exemption from universal ruin, in addition to faith and good deeds, two stringent requirements of faith—exhorting one another to truth and exhorting one another to endurance.

A statement of Prophet Jesus is very helpful in understanding a subtle difference in the subject matter of *Surah At-Teen* and Swift *Al-'Asr.* In the famous Sermon of the Mount he said:

"Go in through the narrow gate; because broad and spacious is the road leading off into destruction, and many are the ones who go in through it; whereas narrow is the gate and cramped the road leading to life, and few are the ones who find it"

Surah At-Teen and *Surah Al-'Asr* both contain a reference to the two paths alluded to by Jesus. The main emphasis of *Surah Al-'Asr* is on that broad path which the large majority of humanity is treading in its blind worship of carnal desires, gratification of sex and hunger, belief in "wishful thinking" and polluted traditions and unauthentic existence, coming nearer every moment to a dreadful end of an eternal doom. On the contrary, the light of *Surah At-Teen* is converging on the other type of path, which, though narrow and followed by a handful of men, ultimately leads to 'openness' and eternal success and well being.

When a thoughtful and sensitive person would think in the light of *Surah Al-'Asr* about the wretched plight of so many and visualize the doom they shall meet, he may well be overwhelmed by a deep sense of dejection and hopelessness. It is just possible that he might lose faith in the natural and primordial goodness of man. In the darkness of this stark pessimism, Surah *At-Teen* appears as a shining ray of hope and confidence. In its light we have a glimpse of some pious and saintly persons following the right path, and also the evidence of man's natural and original goodness and his potential for the pinnacle of excellence. And this quells the darkness of pessimism, giving a man self-confidence and hope about his future.

The universal truth, "Verily man is doomed" has been supported by the equally comprehensive evidence, 'By (the token of time'. This is so because the substantive proposition and its evidence are both almost universal and open to common observation. On the other hand, the rather little known truth expressed in the verse 'Surely we created man in the best of moulds' has been instantiated by a few holy persons who walked under the 'fig and olive trees', or conversed with the Lord on the Mount of Sinai, or were witness to the spiritual greatness of man in the City of Security.

The thundering call of 'By (the token of) time' jolts the mind of a sensitive and thoughtful person out of absorption in his petty personal involvements, and presents to him the vast panorama of world history as unfolded in time. The primary purpose of this adjuration, therefore, is to make the reader ponder over the deeper meaning and value of the vicissitudes of world history.

The truth of the matter is that complete preoccupation with the demands of his immediate environments and personal problems is a manifestation of man's intellectual bankruptcy. In this way the entire expanse of his conscious being is often confined to these demands, and he is rendered incapable of any intuitive illumination emanating from his inner-most self or comprehension of the astounding signs *('ayat'* in Quranic terminology) present throughout the universe. Very insignificant and minor issues of daily life are blown quite out of proportion, and he exhausts all his time and energy in struggling for trifles and petty desires. The Holy Quran has delineated two ways that help a person in coming out of this mental and psychological confinement. First, the way of attaining the ultimate truth through a deep soul-searching, a listening to the affirmations of one's inner self. Second, the way of reflecting and meditating on the signs found in the cosmos and the clear testimonies provided by history. The contents of *Surah Al'Asr* guide us to this latterway.

It is only due to sheer negligence or insensitivity that we take time to be something static. On the contrary, everything, which exists today in the world, will perish before long. Similarly, human beings who are busy now in managing the manifold activities of a full life, will in a matter of few years yield place to other generations. The fleeting passage of time is itself a warning to unmindful persons and should be sufficient to bring home to them that they and all their worldly pursuits will shortly come to an end. Our short lease of life is expiring rapidly, and after a little while we will disappear in the mist of past.

Changes

Time is the greatest teacher and mentor of man. It is labeled in oriental lore as *"Falak-i-Peer"* (the old heaven). In the bosom of time are contained tremendous accounts of nations' rise and fall which can be of great significance and value for people living now on earth. This planet has seen hundreds of nations in the past, rising slowly towards eminence, consolidating their power for sometime and then degenerating and falling into oblivion. How many nations took shape, reached their climax and then vanished without a trace! Dozens of civilizations saw the light of day and, after touching the summit of success and fame, decayed and were annihilated. Billions and billions of human beings were born into this world and after having passed through the stages of adolescence, youth, and old age, returned to dust.

Thousands built big empires by means of massive military campaigns and conquests, some even went to the extent of claiming divine and god-like status for themselves, and ordered their subordinates to worship them. But at last they were all drowned in the ocean of time.

The great historical episodes, alluded to by the Quran in the brief 'By (the token of) time' were studied and expounded in great depth and detail by scholars and commentators of the Holy Book. This particular attempt towards understanding the meaning of the Quran assumed the status of a separate branch of Quranic studies and was termed by Shah Waliullah of Delhi (RA) as *'Tazkeer bi Ayyamillah'* which means reminding or instructing the reader of the Book by means of recounting the moral lessons inherent in the events of past history.

The Quranic verse, 'Verily men are in a state of loss', epitomizes the undeniable tragedy to which relics of history spread all around the world bear witness. The real bitterness of this tragic fact will however be experienced only in the life Hereafter. It is something to be commended that very few persons have been gifted with a really keen and sensitive heart, otherwise thousands of men like Buddha, at the sight of mankind's misery and exceedingly unhappy plight, might have turned their back on worldly pleasures and gone into ascetic hide-outs. On examining rather critically and attentively the human condition, one will come to realize that inspite of hard labour all day long, millions of the unprivileged classes do not even get an adequate meal. There are tens of thousands of people who see their relatives and dear ones dying before their eyes but cannot afford a spoonful of medicine that might help in curing the disease. An unaccountable number of human beings do not possess even the bare minimum of clothing and shelter. Terrible and heart-rending afflictions are suffered by many.

Even the bright exterior of the life of men of privilege and wealth only covers up their own tales of woe. Often the travail and suffering of these men are more dreadful than that of the common run of people. Lnspite of having all conceivable luxuries of life, they crave for an anxiety-free moment during the day and for peaceful sleep at night.

In this stage of terrestrial existence the condition of most men is as pitiable as that of animals which are mercilessly forced to carry back-breaking burdens throughout their life. Taking a more judicious view of things, one can say that pangs of psychic anxiety and bouts of spiritual agony suffered by human beings are much greater in intensity than the purely bodily pains which, animals suffer.

But, still worse, man will see the climax of his tragedy when, having experienced all these worldly hardship, grief and afflictions, he will at last be brought before Almighty Allah for the last reckoning of his deeds. The Quran describes this in these words:

يَا أَيُّهَا الْإِنسَانُ إِنَّكَ كَادِحٌ إِلَىٰ رَبِّكَ كَدْحًا فَمُلَاقِيهِ

'O thou man ! Verily thou art ever toiling on towards thy Lord—painfully toiling--but thou shalt meet Him' [TMQ Surah Tariq: 6]

At that crucial moment of great trial man will cry out:

'Would that I were dust'! The noblest souls of all humanity tremble and quiver at the very thought of that final trial and some men even wish they were like a sparrow chirping on a tree or like a straw of grass (so they might not be called to account for on the day of Judgement).

At that critical moment the reality of the verse 'Verily, man is in a state of loss' will become manifest in the highest degree, and the large majority of human beings will say in utter despair: 'If only my mother had not given birth to me'. As the Quranic verse tells us the most real and obvious loss is the loss met on that Day in the life hereafter.

The last verse of *Surah Al-'Asr* "save those who believe, do good deeds and exhort one another to uphold the truth and exhort one another to constancy", delineates the sole means of deliverance from eternal hell-fire. It is, therefore, imperative that we should exercise utmost diligence in understanding the full meaning of this verse.

Since this verse is inseparably linked with the preceding one "Verily man is in a state of loss", it must be studied principally in this context. Both these verses describe most clearly and distinctly the all-important truth that the success of human life depends upon the following:

1. *'Iman'* or belief (in the metaphysical tenets of Islam).
2. *'Amal-e-Saleh'* or good deeds.
3. 3 *'Twasi bil-Haq'* or mutual exhortation to truth.
4. *'Twasi bis-Sabr'* or mutual exhortation to constancy and steadfastness.

Destruction

Life without fulfilling these four inevitable conditions leads to eternal destruction. However, bright or glittering a man's worldly success might be, it is no success if he lacks the above four conditions. These verses present a criterion of man's ultimate triumph and failure which is diametrically opposed to the one prevalent in present day materialistic society. A thorough grasp of the meaning of these verses and a deep conviction of their veracity must necessarily result in a total transvaluation of values regarding life's aims and achievements. If all that man cherishes most—

political power, social status, affluence, availability of resources, high-ranking posts, well- established business, shining limousines, and big palatial buildings—are unaccompanied by the above mentioned four conditions; then they must be a preamble to eternal torment.

The only thing that can possibly save a man from everlasting doom is a real transformation of his nature, one which reforms his mind and heart and radically changes his perspective to conform to these four items, which collectively constitute the indispensable minimum requirements of human salvation. And this is only sufficient for the deliverance from destruction and not necessarily enough for the attainment of lofty stations in paradise. The Quran is not the work of a poet who says many things simply for the sake of adding elegance to the composition or under the necessity of rhythm and rhyme, but the word of God Almighty, and each word is precise and full of true wisdom. It contains nothing else but *'Haqq'* or the truth, not allowing any addition or diminution whatsoever. If we eliminate even a single of the above mentioned stipulations, the responsibility of the Quran in respect of our salvation stands null and void and it will be sheer self-deception if we consider ourselves as the rightful recipients of the Quranic promise.

Truth

It is most unfortunate that, in the present age of religious degeneration and decline, we have become completely ignorant of this truth. A large majority of Muslims today assumes that belief *(Iman)* is the sole condition of a man's success on the Day of Judgement, and hence takes belief in a strictly legal sense. Those who are a little more sensible and knowledgeable also take good deeds as an essential requirement in addition. But even a good number of learned religious persons nowadays consider 'mutual exhortation to truth' and 'mutual exhortation to constancy and steadfastness' as secondary of supererogatory conditions to be fulfilled only by those desirous of exceptionally higher positions in the Hereafter. May people study and ponder over *Surah Al'Asr* afresh and get to know with full conviction that the Quran has very clearly and unambiguously made human salvation to depend upon four conditions:

1. Belief.
2. Good deeds.
3. Mutual exhortation to uphold the truth, and
4. Mutual exhortation to constancy.

Let us take another step and concentrate our attention on these four points separately so as to get a better comprehension of their profound meaning. The first most important point that comes out on a closer study is that these four things are not to be compared with the four independent items of, for example, a medical compound but rather they are four stages on the road that leads to salvation, four milestones of one single path of truth. They have within themselves an organic unity, and logically imply each other. True belief *(lman)* is a prelude to righteous action which itself is a preliminary to mutual teaching of *truth(Twasi bill-haqq)*. And this in turn is a forerunner of mutual teaching of steadfastness *(Twasi bis-sabr)*.

Deeply entrenched and rightly-nurtured belief and faith must necessarily blossom into righteous life and conduct. Further, if a true believer lived only for himself, he will not have fulfilled his whole duty. Whatever good he possesses, especially moral and spiritual truth, he must disseminate among his brethren, so that they may also see the truth and stand by it in patient hope and unshaken constancy amidst all the storm and stress of worldly life. An essential consequence of righteous life is the teaching of truth to others and this necessitates uniting together and exhorting one another to patience and endurance in facing the forces ofevil.

Reflecting on the reality and pristine nature of faith and belief i.e., *'Iman-* leaving aside its politico-social aspects and legal or theological controversies, we come to know that faith connotes a particular mode of ones s mind or psyche *(nafs* or *qulb)* which is governed by a recognition of the oneness and unity of God, the reality of prophet hood and the life Hereafter. This state of mind reigns over one's entire being, one's faculties of head and heart, so that his desires, emotions and actions all harmonize with this knowledge.

In a word, it does away with disunion and duplicity in cognition and volition, and produces, concordance between them. The essence of genuine belief therefore, lies in a complete co-ordination of a man 's knowledge of ultimate truths and his will and actions. The real fruit of *'Iman'* is the tranquility of mind that a believer experiences as a consequence of this harmony. As long as a man's religious belief remains merely an idea untranslated into action, he will not have attained true belief or *'Iman-* Summing up his excellent discussion of belief Maulana Hamid-ud-Din Farahi writes:

"Belief or *'Iman'* refers to a particular mental and spiritual state which rules over a man's total creed and actions.... it has two pillars : knowledge and action. If we pull down either one of the two, the entire edifice will collapse. A man who is well-versed in theological doctrines such as God's Providence, and in all the principles and details of Islamic faith, but continues to indulge in sinful and forbidden *(haram)* activities, he does not have an iota of that belief or *'Iman'* which alone is creditable in the sight of Allah (SWT).

(Mujmuoe-e-Tafaasir- e-Farahi Page -350)

If this is the nature of faith, then righteous action is a corollary, or, if you prefer, an essential consequence of faith and from the absence of righteous deeds and the actual manifestations of belief, one can rightly infer the lack of faith. A Quranic verse describes this situation thus:

قَالَتِ الْأَعْرَابُ آمَنَّا قُل لَّمْ تُؤْمِنُوا وَلَٰكِن قُولُوا أَسْلَمْنَا وَلَمَّا يَدْخُلِ الْإِيمَانُ فِي قُلُوبِكُمْ
وَإِن تُطِيعُوا اللَّهَ وَرَسُولَهُ لَا يَلِتْكُم مِّنْ أَعْمَالِكُمْ شَيْئًا إِنَّ اللَّهَ غَفُورٌ رَّحِيمٌ

"The desert Arabs say, 'we have faith'. Say Ye have no faith; but ye (only) say, 'We have submitted our wills to God', for not yet has faith entered your hearts. But if ye obey God and his apostle, He will not belittle aught of your deeds for God is Oft- Forgiving, Most Merciful." [TMQ Al Hujurat: 14]

Belief *(Iman)* and righteous deeds are so closely united and inter-twined that the latter can be treated as a *sine qua non* of the former. Indeed to consider the two as one and the same thing is not wholly unjustified.

Understanding the Quranic term *'Amal-i-Saleh'* —righteous or good deeds — requires deep thought and reflection. The Quran includes under this blanket term all its moral and legal teachings, including the laws of individual and social conduct. It also makes an allusion to the fact that the secret of man's real development and progress lies in performing these very acts. Righteous deeds alone can guarantee the growth of man's natural capacities and potentialities on the right lines. To quote Maulana *Farahi* again:

"Almighty Allah has designated good and righteous deeds with the word *'Salehat-* This term itself guides us to the great truth that the whole of man's development and rectitude — be it outward or inner, worldly or spiritual, personal or collective, bodily or intellectual — depends upon good and righteous deeds. Righteous action is life-giving and a source of maturity and enhancement. By means of good deeds alone man can attain those highest stages of development to which he aspires by nature ... This point can be put in alternative words thus: Since man is an integral part of the total scheme of universe, only those of his deeds will be righteous which accord with the grand design on which the universe has been fashioned by its Creator".

Two Sides

And so, belief and faith is simply a complete consonance between a man's true knowledge of the Absolute and his thoughts, ideas, emotions and passions. And righteousness of action is the co- ordination which human actions should have with the Divine will, the will that animates and sustains the cosmos. Belief and righteous deeds are two aspects or facets of one and the same reality, two sides of a single picture. This is the reason why the Quran usually mentions these two together.

There are very few cases in the Quran where belief alone has been mentioned, and even in these cases we can most often, on deeper reflection, discover an implicit reference to the moral and practical obligations that genuine faith must entail.

Let us press our inquiry a step further. It is almost a truism that man is a social animal. There is always an interaction between him and the surrounding social reality. He influences his environment and receives its influence. This can be illustrated by considering an example. Just as fire warms the objects around it while ice freezes what surrounds it, a man's righteous deeds have a wholesome and ennobling influence upon others. Similarly, immoral actions tend to degrade and disintegrate the world. If evil is rampant in a society, a righteous person must struggle hard to ward off its influence. So mutual exhortation to truth *(twasi-bil-haqq)* and mutual exhortation to stead- fastness *(twasi-bis-sabr)* must necessarily ensue from true belief *(Iman)* and righteous deeds. Just as true belief and righteous actions go together, so uniting in truth and in constancy to it are inseparable

Maulana Farahi elaborates the relation between righteous conduct and mutual exhortation

(twasi) in these words

"Just as *'Iman'* gives rise to righteous deeds, so righteous deeds necessarily give rise to mutual encouragement to truth. This is so quite understandably because a person, whose adherence to the truth can make him endure the worst possible trial and affliction, must consider his knowledge of the truth and fidelity to it as superior to everything else".

Truth

He will not rest content merely with his own love of the truth but rather will also wish to see the whole world adhering to it. Wherever he sees the truth trampled upon and falsehood triumphant, he will be moved tremendously, and try to persuade his fellows to support the truth. This defense of his convictions is a natural and essential consequence of his own sentiment. Therefore, Allah has here mentioned *'twasi'* (mutual exhortation) as an implication of *'amal-i-saleh'* (righteous deed). Maulana Farahi has thus explained the literal meaning of the word 'Truth' or *(Haqq)*:

Truth, though originally it signified anything existent, stable, and fixed , in actual usage has acquired a variety of meanings. It is generally used to mean the following three:

(i).Anything the existence or occurrence of which is absolutely sure.
(ii).Anything rationally proved and accepted.

(iii).Any moral obligation.

This amply shows that the expression *'twasi bil-haqq'* (mutual exhortation to truth) covers a wide range of activities starting from the teaching of minor moral duties and the self-evident principles of reason and established facts of the universe, to the highest and most esteemed activity, the propagation and establishment of the religion of truth *(Din-al-Haqq)* which Allah (swt) revealed to the Prophet Muhammad (saw). Maulana Farahi expressed this very explicitly in a passage:

"This brings out clearly the truth that it is incumbent on Muslims to do righteous deeds in order to fulfill their obligations (to the Almighty). This fulfillment further necessitates that they help each other in executing their religious and moral duties. Since execution of all the duties and obligations laid down by Allah (SWT) is not possible without 'Khilafat' (Islamic Government and justice), it is imperative that they strive to establish it"

Now only one step remains to be explored, that mutual exhortation to truth *(twasi-bil-haqq)* necessarily implies mutual exhortation to constancy *(twasi bis-sabr).* Self-restraint and constancy is required even in one's own firm adherence to truth simply because one must exercise self-control in the face of a great many temptations, must curb his sensual appetites, and must face scores of painful disappointments and impediments. At the stage of mutual exhortation to truth *(twasi-bil- haqq)* much bigger trials of patience and resolution become inevitable. It is a matter of common observation that at times even propagating a minor truth puts a man to severe tests of endurance. Sticking to a right policy is sometimes as difficult as trial by fire.

History is replete with instances of torture and wanton injuries inflicted on champions of moral truths. Proclamation and dissemination of the basic truth of man's life and obligation to God may well require proportionately greater ordeals and suffering. If an attempt is made to call all people to the fulfillment of their religious obligations and the establishment of an equitable and just order, severest opposition is sure to follow. Any one may try it for himself. He needs only start by advising people to perform ordinary and simple moral actions, and soon they will frown and become furious. Let him try to persuade somebody who has forcefully usurped the property of a poor man to give the man his due and he will see how great a resentment he must face. Let him just utter a word in support of someone oppressed, and in no time the tyrant becomes his deadly enemy. It should not take much thought to realize that demanding the fulfillment of one's total moral obligations, fighting for an entire system of social justice and equity, and calling to the whole of *'Din-al-Haqq'* (the true religion) can never be possible without utmost hostility and opposition

Unity

If an exhortation is made to uphold the truth without evil forces putting obstacles in its way, if a programmatic and concerted call is issued to establish social justice but tyrants and oppressors merely keep silent, then either the advocates of Truth have some clandestine agreement with the forces of injustice, or they are working for just a part of the Truth, not the whole of it. Men thriving upon injustice may not deem it necessary to suppress a movement towards social justice if they find that that particular part of the truth is harmless to their vested interests. But total commitment to truth and the struggle to establish it inevitably brings persecution and harassment. Every step on this path invites ever greater ordeals and challenges. A poet has rendered this in a beautiful couplet:

"People consider being a true Muslim an easy affair.

Nay! It is like stepping in the pyre of love and martyrdom.

At this stage there is no alternative for men of faith in the true religion but to unite their aspiration and energies. Encouraging and helping each other, being firm and patient themselves and exhorting others to firmness and patience, they must form a united front, what the Quran calls a 'solid cemented structure' In so doing, they will make themselves an embodiment of the Quranic verse:

يَا أَيُّهَا الَّذِينَ آمَنُوا اصْبِرُوا وَصَابِرُوا وَرَابِطُوا وَاتَّقُوا اللَّهَ لَعَلَّكُمْ تُفْلِحُونَ

"*O Ye who believe! persevere in patience and constancy. Vie in such perseverance ; Strengthen each other. And fear God so that ye may succeed and prosper.*"

[TMQ Aal Imran : 200]

At the stage of *'twasi-bil-haqq'* (mutual exhortation to Truth), it is perhaps impossible for Muslims in their individual capacities to stand up to the opposition mounted against them by the evil forces. It is therefore, imperative, that they unite into a well-organized group. This is the reason why the Quran has given the injunctions regarding *'Haqq'* and *'Sabr'* in the Arabic grammatical form of *"tafa'ul'*. that is to say, in the verse *'Wa twaso bil-Haqqe wa twaso bis-sabr'* there is an implicit reference to the necessity of a united and organized group life for Muslims. These virtues we must exercise both for ourselves and in relation to others. We must set an example for others and take the excellence of others as an example for ourselves, so that we may not fall short of what is due from us. In this way we strengthen each other and bind our mutual relations closer in common service to God. In the later part of the passage quoted above from Maulana Farahi's book, he says, '—and since the establishment of *'Khilafat'* depends on obedience to an *'Ameer'* (the leader), it is essential that Muslims submit themselves to discipline. It is, therefore, clear that belief, righteous deeds, mutual exhortation to truth and mutual exhortation to steadfastness are not mutually exclusive. Rather, they are bound together closely in a strictly logical sequence, four stages of a single straight path

Faith is like a seed from which sprouts the bud of righteous conduct. The bud grows into a mature plant with leaves and flowers of mutual exhortation to truth and constancy. This also explains why the Quran almost always couples faith and good deeds, even when only faith is mentioned, the reader can easily understand that it covers in its connotation all of the four requirements. For instance, in the following verse:

إِنَّ الَّذِينَ قَالُوا رَبُّنَا اللَّهُ ثُمَّ اسْتَقَامُوا تَتَنَزَّلُ عَلَيْهِمُ الْمَلَائِكَةُ أَلَّا تَخَافُوا وَلَا تَحْزَنُوا
وَأَبْشِرُوا بِالْجَنَّةِ الَّتِي كُنتُمْ تُوعَدُونَ

'Lo! those who say: Our Lord is Allah, and further stand straight and steadfast....' [TMQ Fussilat: 30]

Here only the most fundamental of Islamic beliefs, *i.e.,* belief in the providence of Almighty Allah, has been mentioned, though, it should be taken to include the other fundamentals, such as Hazrat Muhammad's prophet hood (peace be upon him) and the reality of life in the Hereafter. And in *'Summa-Staqamu'* (further stand straight and steadfast) have been summed up the remaining three conditions, viz., righteous conduct, mutual exhortation of truth and mutual exhortation to persistence in truth. At other places in the Quran, in addition to the primal condition of belief only mutual exhortation has been mentioned. The following verse of *Surah 'Al.-Balad'is* an example of this:

ثُمَّ كَانَ مِنَ الَّذِينَ آمَنُوا وَتَوَاصَوْا بِالصَّبْرِ وَتَوَاصَوْا بِالْمَرْحَمَةِ

"Then will he be of those who believe and enjoin compassion".

[TMQ Balad: 17]

The truth of the matter is that all these four conditions are basic to the Quranic way that leads to eternal bliss and salvation. Elucidation and explanation of these requirements and detailed accounts of their stages and degrees are found throughout the Holy Book.

Conditions

In the preceding paragraph mention has been made of stages and degrees pertaining to the several conditions of success and salvation. A point of crucial importance as it is, a few brief remarks about them are in order here. Each of the three articles of belief, righteous deeds and mutual exhortation of truth admits of degrees and ranks. Taking belief first, even the ordinary believer who accepts faith, that is who believes in the tenets of Islam and does good deeds, becomes a member of a great and beautiful spiritual fraternity — a company which lives perpetually in the sunshine of God's grace.

Within itself however *'Iman'* has a glorious hierarchy, of which two grades are specified by the Quran: the highest grade is that of the prophets, who get plenary inspiration from Allah (SWT) and who teach mankind by example and precept and that of the 'Siddiqeen', the most sincere lovers of truth, who support the truth with their person, their means, their influence, and all that is theirs. This second rank was held by the closest companions of Prophet Muhammad (SAW), such as *Hazrat Abu Bakr Siddique* (RAA).

Similarly the category of righteous deed *(amal-i-saleh)* applies to a wide variety of actions, beginning from the very ordinary moral acts of kindness like removing a stone from a road on which men walk. In its higher reaches it is attributable to thorough obedience to Quranic injunctions covering all aspects of a Muslim's life, including even the minor details of his personal life. It means more than just conformity to an external code of law. At its highest level it permeates all actions to attain a state of moral excellence which the Quran calls *'ihsan'* and *'taqwa'*.

In a like manner *'twasi bil-haqq'* has several grades. Its lowest stage is exhorting one another to perform acts of kindness and compassion, *'twasi bil-marhama'*, on occasions which arise fairly commonly in every day life. A sense of kindness and compassion has been ingrained in the nature of human beings and only the most wicked one lacks it. According to a Quranic verse, those who discourage or forbid others from feeding the poor have touched the nadir of moral depravity.

Kindness

A prophetic saying further elaborates this in these words: 'He who is devoid of kindness is devoid of all good'.

A higher stage of *'twasi bil-haqq'* is that of calling people to Allah, enjoining good and forbidding evil. A true Muslim should give clothing to the ill-clad, food to the hungry and drink to the thirsty. But the greatest benefit he can render to his fellow beings is to turn them back from moral and spiritual bankruptcy and guide them to the straight path of the Quran and Sunnah. In one's life journey to the ultimate goal, the duty of each Muslim is to catch hold of the hand of one who goes astray from the straight path of Islam and to guide him aright. Mutual counsel gives life to actions and foster a healthy spirit among the individuals.

At a still higher stage, *'twasi bil-haqq'* adopts the form of testifying to the truth and veracity of Islam *(Shahadat-ihaqq)* exalting the truth from Allah over all man-made ideologies *(E'Ia-e- Kallmatillah),* and establishing Islam both in the individual and social aspects of life *(Iqamat-i-Din).* The testimony to the truth may be by the tongue of a true preacher or the pen of a devoted scholar, or by the life of a man devoted to service. The highest and most revered form of this testimony is presented by a Muslim who leaves his house and family to fight the enemy for the cause of Allah *(Jehad-fi-Sabilillah).* Endurance is the greatest solace of a true Muslim while going through all the trials on account of *'twasi bil-haqq'*. Especially in the higher stages, mutual teaching and exhorting to constancy become so essential that *'twasi-bis-sabr'* has been mentioned separately to highlight the collective and cooperative character of Muslim society.

It is no doubt difficult for all and sundry to attain the above mentioned highest stages of belief or *'Iman',* righteous deeds, mutual exhortation of truth and mutual exhortation of patience and endurance. But if a man's inner personality has not been corroded by some spiritual or moral ailment, it is almost certain that a healthy and potent seed of religious belief will flourish into wholesome and balanced branches of righteous actions, exhortation to truth and constancy.

It is surely excusable if a lay Muslim, who has very little knowledge of the fundamentals of Islam and performs the well known basic duties of *'Shariah'* (Islamic code of law), confines himself to *'twasi bil-marhama'* i.e., doing himself acts of kindness and compassion and advising others to the same, which is just the threshold of *'twasi bil-Haqq'*. But those who embark on rigorous spiritual exercises like repeated recitation of a religious formula called *'Zikr'* to attain deeper and richer states of faith and belief, those who engage themselves in devotional prayers and *'mustahabbat'* (some thing additional to what is obligatory of *'farz')* but pay little attention to the more obligatory duty of *'twasi- bil-haqq'* are seriously misguided in their attitude.

Lives of these people are mostly either totally devoid of the essential religious duty of *'twasi bll-haqq'* or they exhibit just a vestige of it in the form of occasional brief sermon or sporadic moralizing advice. This state of affairs is certainly wrong and needs to be rectified immediately. In this connection a story reported by Prophet Muhammad (peace be upon him) puts the urgency of this duty in very bold relief. He mentioned an extremely pious old man whom the angels testified that he never indulged in sin even for as long as the blink of an eye, but who never angered or got moved at the sight of people breaking the commands of God. Despite all his piety and life-long spiritual observances, Allah ordered the angels to destroy him first and then the entire community.

On the other hand, it should also be clearly understood that it is equally dangerous to aspire and struggle for the highest stages of *'twasi bil-haqq'* through activities geared to establishing an Islamic order of society, but taking meager interest in spiritual devotions and performing only those prayers which are obligatory *(farz),* and attenuate faith to a mere theological belief without realizing its deeper meaning and cultivating it inwardly. All types of unbalanced attitudes and life-styles within these two extremes are misconceived and possibly dangerous.

Struggle

The sole way of salvation and deliverance from eternal damnation towards which *Surah Al-'Asr* points is that every human being should strive and struggle within the limits of his capacity to attain the maximum degree of faith, righteous action, enjoinment of truth and of constancy. As far as the question of determining one's capacities is concerned, there is a simple and foolproof procedure for this which each may apply to himself.

Self deceiving and self-pitying excuses of incapability may be induced by *Satan (Devil),* but the honest test of self-assessment is quite simply this: each Muslim should ask himself to what extent he is exerting himself in the economic struggle of life and to what degree his capacities and potentialities, mental and physical, are becoming visible in the over-all course of mundane pursuits. If a weak, frail and ungifted person who has either met complete failure or lagged far behind in the struggle of worldly existence tenders on the Day of Judgement some excuse for his shortcoming and deficiency in spiritual attainments, he is most likely to be pardoned by the Grace of Allah. But surely those who are progressing and flourishing in worldly matters cannot legitimately make such excuses. Nor should they expect from Allah any mercy on them. A Quranic verse puts this unambi- guously in these words:

يَقُولُ الْإِنسَانُ يَوْمَئِذٍ أَيْنَ الْمَفَرُّ – وَلَوْ أَلْقَىٰ مَعَاذِيرَهُ

"Nay, man will be a telling witness against himself, even though he were to put forward excuses!' [TMQ Al Qiyamah:14, 15]

Commentary On Surah Al-'Asr

(A speech delivered at Aitchison College, Lahore)

Four Fundamental Points Regarding Surah Al-'Asr:

1. The first point is that this is one of the earliest surahs of the Glorious Quran to be revealed. It was revealed to Prophet Muhammad (peace be upon him) in the earliest period of his prophet hood in Makkah.
2. The second point is that it is one of the shortest *surahs* of the Glorious Quran as it has only three verses, the first of which is comprised of only one word *"Wal-Asr"*.
3. The third point is that it is one of the most comprehensive *surahs* of the Glorious Quran. The Holy Quran is a book of guidance for all mankind, which has been revealed to guide mankind on the road to success and salvation. This path of salvation towards which the Holy Quran guides us has been described with utmost brevity and comprehensiveness in this short *surah*.

The whole Glorious Quran is like a tree, and this short *surah* is its seed. And as a seed contains the total potentiality of a whole tree, *Surah Al-'Asr* contains the essence of the Holy Quran.

This is why some reports of the Companions of the Holy Prophet (may Allah be pleased with them) indicate that whenever two of them met and sat together they never parted without reciting *Surah Al-'Asr* to each other.

And this can be the reason why *Imam Al-Sha'feii* (may Allah bless him) has said about this *surah* that if the people were to ponder over this *surah* alone, it would suffice for their guidance. He has also been reported as saying that if nothing else would have been revealed in this Glorious Quran except this *surah* then this *surah* would have been sufficient for man's guidance.

4. The fourth point is that the wording of this *surah* is very simple and easy to understand. The masterpieces of literature of every language are sublime in subject matter and meaning but so simple in style and wording that they can be understood by all. This is why such pieces of literature are easily accessible to everyone. The Glorious Quran is the most eminent masterpiece of Arabic literature and in its totality can be understood easily. But this short *surah* is the best example of the most lucid *surahs* of the Holy Quran. Though it is very complete and all-embracing, not a single high-sounding or elusive word has been used in it. Its words are familiar even to those who are only acquainted with Urdu or Persian, and do not know Arabic.

The Two Levels of Understanding Quran:

Before describing the significance of this *surah,* it is important to state the fundamental principle that the Quran can be comprehended on many levels. The real lesson which is implicit in any *surah* or verse of the Holy Quran should be made explicit in order that the basic guidance regarding hu- man conduct may be attained. The Glorious Quran calls this *Tazakkur-bil-Quran, i.e.,* realizing through the Quran the fundamental truths implicit in human nature. From this point of view, the Glorious Quran is the easiest of books to understand. The highest stage of contemplation of Quranic verses has been termed *Tadabbur-i-Quran,* which means reflecting and pondering over every word deeply, in order to deduce the philosophy and the wisdom of the Holy Book. In this sense the Holy Quran is the most difficult of books as it is not easy to attain the depth of its meaning.

In this paper, I will describe clearly and in detail the basic guidance obtained through the application of *Tazakkur-bil Quran* to *Surah Al-'Asr.* I will also include some hints concerning *Tadabbur-i-Quran* so that those who are interested in the deeper contemplation of the Quran may also benefit.

The English Translation of Surah Al-'Asr:

A simple translation of the *surah* is as follows:

1. *By Time,*
2. *Verily all human beings are in loss,*
3. *Except those who have achieved 'Faith', have performed Righteous deeds, and have emphasized to each other the teaching of 'Truth' and (the value of) 'Patience' (perseverance and constancy).*

Analysis of the Translation:

The three verses in this *surah* form one complete sentence. The first verse *"Wal-'Asr"* is an oath. The second verse describes a general rule. The third verse describes an exception from that general rule. Combined together, all the three verses constitute a single statement.

Please implant this simple statement firmly and clearly in your mind. And by pondering over it, you should deduce four conclusions which are the basic lessons of this *surah.*

The Criterion of Success and Failure:

The most important truth flowing forth from this *surah* is Allah's presentation of the real criterion of man's success and failure.

Every person keeps in his mind a criterion of success and failure, of gain and loss. All his endeavours and the whole struggle of his life in this world is directed according to this criterion. An intellectually mature person is rarely found who does not have an appointed goal or an ideal before him. Even small children, specially the more intelligent ones, keep before them a standard of achievement. They concentrate their energies on the attainment of their goals.

If we were to look around in our society as well as to search our hearts and minds, we would find that in this age, the real criterion of success or failure is wealth and property, or status, honour, fame and ostentation, or worldly power. All but a few are running after these things. They expend their energies for these purposes. The minds of most of our students are directed towards obtaining degrees in science or technology, so that they may earn a lot of money or achieve status, position or power. The achievement of these things is their criterion of success or failure.

The paramount truth which comes to our minds by studying *Surah Al-'Asr* is very different from this. In other words, the criterion of man's success is neither money or wealth, nor status, position, power, or ostentation. Rather its first condition is 'Faith', the second is 'righteous deeds', the third is 'exhortation to truth', and the fourth is 'exhortation to patience'.

By this criterion, a person who does not possess the above four qualities is unsuccessful and will never achieve his real goal, and in the end he will be a loser, though he might be a millionaire, even a billionaire like Qarun and might have highest status, position, and power, even kingship like Pharaoh or Herod. Conversely any one who has these four prerequisites is successful and triumphant, even if he has no worldly wealth or property, and may be penniless, homeless, friendless, unknown, unhonoured and starving.

If you reflect deeply over it, you will find that acknowledging this truth is very easy, but its realization in your heart and soul is very difficult. We are living in a world of cause and effect, and we are bound to be influenced by its external features. When we see that comfort, prosperity, honour and reputation is due to wealth and worldly resources, we involuntarily rush to get these things, so much so that we forget to distinguish between right and wrong, legal and illegal, approved and forbidden. In other words, the reformation of our attitudes and the righteousness of our actions depends upon changing our criteria of our success and failure, gain and loss. This is the real lesson of this unique *surah.*

With a little contemplation it will become clear that if the simple truth stated in this great surah is engraved on our heart and penetrates our soul, it will revolutionize our point of view, change our values, and transform radically our day to day life. What was thought most important before will appear to be most trivial, and what was insignificant before will become significant.

The great transformation which was brought about in the lives of the Companions of the Holy Prophet Muhammad (peace be upon him) was the result of this deep-rooted change in their point of view. In their sight this world arid whatever is in it seemed insignificant as compared to the achievement of Allah's pleasure and that of the Prophet. This is the real lesson of this magnificent *surah,* and everyone should keep it in mind so that it may be infused in his heart and soul.

The Minimum Conditions and Essential prerequisites of Salvation:

This *surah* describes only the minimum conditions and the essential prerequisites for salvation, not the highest stages of achievement, nor the lofty ranks of success and accomplishment. It explains the minimum demanded of us for our salvation. Anything less would be failure. It does not mention first or second division, grades 'A' or 'B' of success, but only states the mere passing grade, the minimum requirement for our success.

This second conclusion has very important implications for our actions. The extreme decadence of the moral and practical life of Muslims is a result of their forgetting this injunction of the Glorious Quran. The realization that this is the minimum standard of success will necessarily produce the proportionate effort, struggle, and sacrifice for achieving it. People who strive for the lofty ranks and sublime stages of religious excellence are rare. Most men only try to fulfil the minimum requirements for salvation in one way or another. This is why in this glorious *surah* the minimum demands of salvation have been described in simplest terms so that people may dedicate themselves to its achievement according to their capability.

All the four Conditions are indispensable:

The third conclusion is a corollary of the second one. For salvation, 'faith', 'righteous deeds', 'exhortation of truth', and 'exhortation of patience' are all necessary. None of them can be dropped. These are the words of Allah. Not a single additional word is added in it for the sake of rhyme or exaggeration. Four conditions have been stated for saving us from utter loss or failure, and certainly all four of them are necessary. If any one of them is left out, then the guarantee of man's salvation will not rest on the Holy Quran. For example, if a medical expert writes four medicines in a prescription for a patient, and the patient leaves out any of them according to his own judgement, then the medical expert will not be responsible for the incomplete medication. The patient himself will be responsible for this error.

It is necessary to emphasize this fact, because a false notion has taken hold of the great majority of Muslims that salvation depends on the mere utterance of the declaration of 'faith, that the mere verbal confession of 'faith' is sufficient for salvation, and any practical application of it to his life is an additional goodness which will elevate him to high stages. You will find very few people who think that after professing faith actively living by its dictates is necessary for salvation. Even these few people rarely regard it as necessary for everyone to take up the task of 'exhortation to truth'. It is usually assumed that the propagation of the message of Islam is the task of a particular group only, and for others preaching is neither necessary nor suitable. Even that special group, instead of propagating the complete truth facing all the tribulations this effort brings with it, have left the path of determination and sacrifice, and made their path easier by attenuating Allah's requirements. In this manner the whole Muslim Nation has become dominated by inactivity, stagnation, escapism, and sloth. This situation cannot change until Muslims realize that the performance of righteous deeds is essential for salvation. Even more is required. The affirmation and declaration of truth and inviting others to accept it, as well as remaining steadfast in the face of hardships and calamities for truth's sake is also necessary. This is the truth which has been stated in this shortest but most comprehensive *surah.*

It is necessary to understand the rational relation between these four components. To be called a man of character implies, judging what is wrong or right in every matter, then adopting in practice whatever his heart and mind has sanctioned as right. A man must not only adopt it himself, but must declare it openly, inviting others to acknowledge and accept it. If in this connection, he faces difficulties and hardships, or has to offer sacrifices, then he must show courage and fortitude, patience and perseverance, and should never retreat or withdraw from his stand. For a man of noble character, it is not possible to adopt any other course. Otherwise he will be a coward and man of weak character, not a man of principle. This is the rational and logical sequence in these four components: (1) 'faith' (2) 'righteous deeds' (3) 'exhortation to truth' (4) 'exhortation to patience and endurance'. And it is not possible for a man of strong character to try to avoid any one of these.

Eloquence with categorical Emphasis:

The fourth conclusion obtained by analyzing and paraphrasing this *surah* is that the above three conclusions are categorical and most emphatic in their nature and that there is no doubt concerning any of them. Our whole faith rests upon accepting the Glorious Quran as the word of Allah and accepting this word as infallible. And who can be more truthful in his statements than Allah? Moreover, Allah has not merely stated these truths, but has taken an oath for confirming their validity. This oath makes this statement more emphatic, and whatever realities are hidden in it, and whatever moral lessons are conveyed by it, are all of them delivered with complete certainty, free from all doubts and compromise. This means that mankind is unknowingly moving towards utter loss and is on the verge of destruction, with the exception of those who have fulfilled these four conditions of 'faith', 'righteous deeds', 'exhortation to truth', and 'exhortation to patience', and ha passed all tests and ordeals which come in the way of fulfilling these conditions.

These are the four basic conclusions which can be drawn by contemplating on this glorious *surah.* In fact this is the gist of *Surah Al-'Asr,* according to the practice of *Tazakkur-bil-Quran* in order to obtain its basic meaning.

Now I want you to study and understand every word of this *surah* rather in depth, in order to make clear that inspire of its simple wording great realities are concealed in it, and gems of wisdom and prudence are hidden in it.

The Real Meaning of "Wal-'Asr":

Let us take the word "*Wal-'Asr*" which we have simply translated as 'taking an oath by time'.

The real meaning of *'Asr'* is not only time, but a period which passes swiftly. In Arabic language the two words *'Asr'* ( )and *'Dahr'* ( ) are very comprehensive. In both of them, not only time, but time-space complex is implied. Curiously enough in the Glorious Quran, there are *surahs* with the title of both *'Asr'* and *'Dahr*. The word *'Dahr'* connotes the vastness of the space-time continuum, or in the terminology of modern philosophy, absolute time or pure duration. The word *'Asr'* connotes the sweep of time or its swift flow. In other words, *'Asr'* means serial time.

In the word *"Wal-'Asr"* the letter 'و ' *(wa'w)* is a preposition, and is used as an oath and testimonial. In short, the real meaning of the word *"Wal-'Asr"* is that the swift passage of time through the ages bears witness and provides evidence for the statements that follow.

The Vast Meaning of *'Khusran'* or Loss:

We have translated the second verse as 'Verily all human beings are in loss'. But even this translation does not convey the real meaning, because the Quranic term *'Khusran'* is not a monetary loss of a few thousands or millions, but indicates complete destruction, in the Holy Quran many words have been used for achievement and success such as accomplishment, triumph, fulfillment, and blessing. But as an antonym of all these, only one comprehensive word is used and that is *'Khusran* It means that the second verse really shows that the whole mankind is standing on the verge of destruction or doom.

The significant reality which has been described in this verse, and the human tragedy towards which this verse points out, can be conceived or realized full in its true perspective in two stages.

Firstly, every one in this worldly life faces a hard struggle for existence. Many people have to undertake rigorous labour from morning till evening, but are unable to provide the bare necessities of life for their dependents. The majority of human beings can not afford even the basic necessities of life, such as food, clothing, shelter, education, and medical care. Even prosperous people have to work hard to maintain their status. From this point of view, a human being is like a beast of burden. But it is even more tragic because he is a creature of feelings and emotions. In addition to all that labour, he has to bear numerous mental hardships. Sometimes, he is deeply moved by the love of his children, sometimes by the troubles faced by his kith and kin. Sometimes he has to put up with the sorrow of a relative's illness, or the shock of the death of someone loved by him. Not only hard work and labour is his lot but grief and sorrow as well.

You must have known that by observing these very troubles and tribulations of life Buddha was so much disheartened and dismayed that in the prime of his life he left his young wife and innocent son and ran out to the jungles in search of 'truth'.

The masses generally harbour the misunderstanding that wealthy and prosperous people have no anxieties. As a matter of fact, the kind of psychic agony which they face is rarely experienced by a common man. They face numerous conflicts and frustrations, and very often the people of this class fall prey to mental diseases and psychic disorders. This is the first stage of human tragedy and this has been mentioned very eloquently in the last part of the Glorious Quran, is *surah* No. 90 *'Al-Balad'* in verse No. 4 wherein Allah says:

'Verily We have created man in toil and struggle.'

But added to this tragedy of the terrestrial existence I the doom of the worst type that is manifest in the life Hereafter. The climax of human tragedy is that after tolerating all troubles and hardships of this world, suddenly he will have to present himself before his Creator and give account for all the activities of his life. This is the picture. which has been presented in *surah* No. 84, entitled *'Insheqaq'* verse No. 6 wherein Allah says:

'Verily O man, thou art ever toiling on towards thy Lord —painfully toiling — but thou shalt meet Him'.

And, if in that trial, his thoughts, convictions, actions and activities are found deviating from the straight path, he would undergo a heart-rending and most severe punishment and torture in the hell for ever. And this is the real loss as Allah says in the Holy Quran:

'That is the sheer loss'

The Inter-relation of the First Two Verses:

It is clear that the first verse is an oath and the second is the statement for which the oath has been taken. That is, in the second verse a truth has been stated, and in the first evidence has been presented for it. The question is: what is the logical sequence between the two?

By contemplating over it, we realize that 'time', constantly passing, is like a sheet, which is spread up to eternity. It means that 'time' is an entity, which is an eye witness to the entire passage of man's life, from his birth to death and to the life of the Hereafter. Hence, the toiling, painful life of man is present before it, and it stands witness also to the momentous events of the rise and fall of nations. The life of the Hereafter, the climax of human tragedy, is also before its gaze. Thus 'time' is the greatest witness to the fact that 'verily man is in a state of loss.

This ascertained truth has an added element of warning implied by *"Wal-'Asr'* This warning is, that the real cause of mankind's ruination, destruction, and utter loss is his negligence, and that by entangling himself in his immediate problems and the trivial affairs of his life, he faces a state of perplexity and self-negation.

The word *"Wal-'Asr"* is a clarion call to wake him up from his indifference and slumber. It points out: O careless man! your real asset is time, which is passing swiftly, and your real capital is this probationary period of worldly life which is ending quickly, and if you are unable to build up your personality, or according to the words of lqbal, the poet of the East, if you have not achieved any sublimity in your SELF or EGO, then you will have 'to face eternal loss, and your life will be doomed.

The Real Meaning of *'Iman'* or Faith:

The first condition of salvation, or deliverance from this sheer destruction, is *'Iman'* (faith). The word *'Iman'* has been derived from *'aman'* meaning peace. Its literal meaning is to provide peace and tranquillity But in its technical sense the word *'Iman'* is used with the prepositions (ل) or (ب) such asor . In this form its literal meaning is to have trust or in and to testify. In order to understand the real meaning of *'Iman'* (faith) it is necessary to realize that any man who has attained maturity of intelligence obviously starts thinking on perennial questions like "Who am I '?", "From where did I come ?", "What is the nature of the Universe ?" and "What is the last destination of the journey of my life ?" Those who have studied philosophy, know that throughout the history of human thought many thinkers continued to ponder over these questions, and tried to find satisfactory answers. Without an answer to these questions, a human being is in the dark, knowing little about his real self, or about the universe, or his own beginning, or the beginning or end of the Universe.

It is evident that these questions cannot be answered merely by our physical senses. As yet we have not been able to fathom the vastness even of the physical world. How can we have any knowledge of its beginning or end? Similarly, the question whether or not we had any existence before our creation in this world, and whether after death there will be any continuity of our existence or not, cannot be answered by our senses, because we cannot possibly peep into the world of existence either prior to our birth or beyond physical death. In short, man is utterly helpless to attain true and ultimate knowledge.

Despite these natural limitations, there have been in the history of mankind a number of persons who claimed that they had a special source of knowledge which they called 'revelation'. On the authority of 'revelation' they knew for certain that this universe did not exist from eternity nor would to remain in existence for ever. It has been brought into existence by a Creator Who possesses all the attributes of perfection in their utmost degree of excellence, and He is Unique in His essence and attributes. He had always existed and will continue to exist for ever. It is He Who has created you, and your life is not the life of this world only, but He would again bring you back to life after death, and that life will be real and eternal. In that life of the Hereafter, you will face your rewards or punishments for your convictions, actions and pursuits during this life. This Creator and Master has assigned messengers from among men and given them the task of proclaiming these verities and the right way of living in this world so that men may be saved from sheer loss in the life Hereafter and may achieve success and eternal bliss.

These Messengers are known as Prophets of Allah and the affirmation of our belief in them is called *'Iman'* or belief in prophethood. This faith has two aspects: verbal confession and certainty in our hearts. We testify verbally that we believe in all prophets, and, according to their teachings, we believe in Allah with all His revealed attributes, and we believe in life after death, and in the day of judgement, in reward and punishment, and in hell and heaven. We also accept these verities with utmost certitude in our hearts. These two conditions constitute our faith or *'Iman'* Faith is certitude about the Creator, man and the universe. It leads to two results:

The first is that a man's internal anxiety must disappear and he must achieve inner peace and satisfaction, when, as a result of this faith, the natural inquisitiveness regarding his own identity and the nature of universe is gratified. This internal serenity is the gift of faith. That is why, etymologically, the Arabic word for faith is a derivative of the root word *'aman'* which means peace.

The second is a reform of one's actions and life-style. As the Socratic doctrine says 'Knowledge is virtue, and ignorance is vice'. A believer should be adorned with high morals and virtuous deeds, and should be free from inferior and degrading actions.

This second point is very important because it shows that 'faith' and 'action' are linked, that faith *(Iman)* and righteous deeds *(Amal-i-Saleh)* are interrelated. Compare for a moment two men. One thinks that this universe has come into existence accidentally and that its entire system and organization is running automatically. The second acknowledges that there is an Almighty, All- knowing, All-wise, All-powerful, Supreme Being, Who has ordained and created this cosmos and that He is the Ordained Who has ordained this Universe and everything in it, and it is running according to His decrees. Is it possible that the life attitude and actions of these two persons would be similar? Would not there be a tremendous difference between their attitudes and behaviour? Similarly, one man thinks that this life which he is leading in this world is the only life and there is no life after death, there is no accountability, no responsibility, no reward or punishment. Another man is sure that the real and everlasting life will begin after death, that the life of this material world is nothing but a preamble of that real life which will start in the Hereafter, and that after death every person will be answerable not only for every action, but for every word and thought. The attitudes and actions of these two would necessarily be different.

It is quite easy to conclude that the goal of life of the former would be to enjoy every minute of this life, as there is no life after it. And in this gratification of the instinct of enjoyment, he might not distinguish between right and wrong, lawful and unlawful. But the second man would take every step in his life with caution and he would be conscious of his responsibility at all times. A man's faith necessitates tremendous transformation in his life.

Please do understand clearly that the idea commonly held in our society that 'faith' and 'action' are separate is only true about the legal aspect of 'faith'. In this society a man is considered and pronounced a Muslim on the basis of verbal confession only. We cannot possibly include his action and conduct in this. But that genuine 'faith' which includes certainty of one's heart and soul must bring a transformation in one's actions. If one's daily life is not changed, this is an absolute proof that genuine 'faith' does not exist in his heart. His faith is no more than a profession.

This truth has been clarified by the Holy Prophet Muhammad (peace be upon him) in many of his traditions and sayings. He said:

"A man who betrays his trust has no 'faith', and the person who does not fulfil his promise has no religion."

Now think over it and see how beautiful is our Prophet's way of expression, and how the thought expressed is as clear as a basic mathematical proposition.

Similarly, once the Prophet of Islam (peace be upon him) swore three times, saying:

"By God, he is not a believer, by God, he is not a believer, by God, he is not a believer". The Companions of the Prophet enquired: "Who is that person about whom you are saying this

?" He said in reply "It is the person from whose misconduct his neighbour is not safe."

Just see how emphatically the Holy Prophet has referred to the complete negation of faith and that too not on account of committing a major sin, such as, polytheism, unjustified murder, adultery, theft or robbery, but only on account of something normally regarded as merely poor behaviour. Is there any justification after this for thinking that 'faith' and 'action' are separate things and are not co-essential and interrelated? This is why in order to remove this misunderstanding completely the Holy Quran consistently mentions righteous deeds as the accompaniment of 'faith'.

So long as faith is confined to the stage of verbal confession and it is limited upto an utterance of words only, actions can be exactly the opposite of it, because the contradiction of word and actions is very commonly found in this world. But when faith reaches a state of certainty in our heart, when it penetrates our heart and soul and becomes an unshakable conviction, then our actions will necessarily be changed because the actions of a man are based on his belief and conviction. For example, we know that fire can burn us, so we would never put even a finger in it. Even suspicion can influence our actions. We know that all snakes are not poisonous, but still even if we suspect that a particular snake might be poisonous, we keep away from it. Now if a person believes with utmost surety that Allah exists and that He is All-seeing, All-hearing, All-knowing; that every movement of his, every word which he utters and, more than this, even every intention of his heart is known to Him; that after death, he shall have no alternative but to present himself before Him, and shall have to give full account of his entire life, with no chance of escaping from the grip of His punishment, nor any hope of deliverance through ransom or intercession; then that man, believing all these things firmly, would not dare to lead a sinful life. This is the condition which has been described in the following saying of Prophet Muhammad (SAW):

"No adulterer commits adultery while he has faith. No thief commits a theft while he has faith. And no drunkard drinks intoxicants while he has faith."

In fact these sins are committed only at a time when due to one reason or another the real faith of a man has dissipated or vanished from his heart. Faith and righteous deeds are interdependent and each of them is essential for the other. Righteous deeds, good morals and a lofty character are *sine qua non* of true faith. This is why in *Surah Al-'Asr',* after faith, righteous deeds have been mentioned as a necessary condition of salvation.

The Real Meaning of Righteous Deeds:

The phrase righteous deeds is commonly translated as good actions. But, if we look deep into it, we would discover more significance hidden behind it. The two locutions 'action' and 'activity' are generally taken to convey the same sense. But there is a subtle difference in their meaning. Any kind of movement or work can be called activity, but the word action usually implies some strenuous or arduous work. On the other side, the word 'virtuous' or 'righteous' denotes something which had developmental characteristics and potential for enhancement. By combining these two, we would realize that the actual significance of this term is that it is necessary for man to put up a hard struggle to achieve that real goat for which he was potentially created, and he had to ascend certain heights to attain that goal. All this is conveyed by the comprehensive word 'righteous deed'.

Surah 'At-Teen' in many respects resembles *Surah Al'Asr.* Verses 4, 5 and 6 of the *surah* state:

لَقَدْ خَلَقْنَا الْإِنسَانَ فِي أَحْسَنِ تَقْوِيمٍ – ثُمَّ رَدَدْنَاهُ أَسْفَلَ سَافِلِينَ – إِلَّا الَّذِينَ آمَنُوا
وَعَمِلُوا الصَّالِحَاتِ فَلَهُمْ أَجْرٌ غَيْرُ مَمْنُونٍ –

'Surely we created man of the best stature. Then we reduced him to the lowest of the low, save those who believe and do good works, and theirs is a reward unfailing.' [TMQ At-Teen: 4-6]

This means that, in reality, man was created for the most sublime rank, and Allah conferred on him superiority not only over *Jinn* (Genie) but also over angels. He was even endowed with the vicegerency of God. But in his terrestrial existence the spiritual self is imprisoned in his gross body of clay, wherein he falls a prey to the clutches of his carnal nature and is reduced to the lowest of low. Now to regain his lost status and sublime rank, it is necessary for him to obtain real knowledge. He must illumine his inner self with the light of faith and must perform good deeds, adorning his outer self with righteous actions, observing the canonical law of Islam and following the Prophet's way of life. These are the prime prerequisites of his salvation.

The Meaning of Mutual Exhortation:

In the last part of *Surah Al- 'Asr,* the word *'tawasau'* has been used twice. Its verbal noun is *'tawasi'* and it is derived from *'wasiyyat'* which means admonition, exhortation with persistent emphasis. Again, this infinitive is formed from the stem of the verbal noun *'tafaul',* whose first attribute is mutual cooperation and the second is emphasis to the point of exaggeration. It means that this action of exhortation is required with the greatest fervour and intensity. This stage necessitates the establishment of a collective community or Ummah based on the principles of mutual preaching of truth and patience.

The Meaning of 'Haqq' or Truth:

Similarly, the connotation of the word *'Haqq' is* very extensive. Its meaning includes everything which is actually real (that is, it is not imaginary or based on presumption). It also connotes what is acknowledged by reason or is necessary ethically, or is purposive and not useless or vacuous. Hence exhortation to truth means confirming, acknowledging, inviting to and preaching every thing which is factually true and real, is ethically necessary and is proved by reason. Thus the spectrum of 'truth' encompasses on the one hand the testimony of the evident facts of our existence and, on the other hand, the testimony of the ultimate metaphysical truths of existence. Exhortation to truth includes a whole range of activities, from giving personal moral advice to the clarion call of the greatest truth, the truth that the real Lord and master of this universe is Allah, and that it is He who deserves that His Commands should be promulgated and that His laws should be enforced in this world. And this truth should not merely be pronounced verbally, but a vigorous struggle should be launched for its practical implementation and actualization.

Similarly, the comprehensive term 'exhortation to truth' embraces within itself concepts which underlie many technical terms of the Holy Quran, such as preaching virtues and holding back people from vices. It implies asking and inviting people to do good deeds and stop them from falling in the snare of every kind of evil, exhorting them to be merciful, to have compassion for each other and to be kind to each other; and calling people towards Allah, persuading them to seek real knowledge and devotion before their Real Sovereign and Master, Allah. Also it includes efforts in the path of Allah, that is, struggling hard for the establishment of the supremacy of the true religion of Allah and spending one's wealth for this purpose and sacrificing one's life for this noble cause.

The Meaning of Patience:

The meaning of patience is very comprehensive. Its real essence is that a person should continue to maintain himself upon the chosen path, without allowing any trouble, or temptation to deviate him from it. No amount of persecution or trial should cause him to desist. He must remain steadfast in every situation, and should display firmness, perseverance, bravery and fortitude. He must not only persevere in following the truth but must also continue to persuade others to accept it and comply with it.

Exhortation to Truth and Exhortation to Patience are co-essential:

As faith and righteous deeds are inter-related; so are exhortation to truth and exhortation to patience. This is because the invitation to truth is usually not welcomed and it has often to face resistance. It is necessary for those who are dedicated to truth to put up with oppression and persecution.

Perhaps all of us have experienced that even a little piece of moral advice can be disliked by people. For example, if a person owes five dollars to some one, and is putting off its payment and you ask him to pay that amount to his creditor, he will frown at you. If he is in an angry mood, he may warn you not to interfere in his affairs. Now you can well imagine how much resistance would be offered and to what extent people will oppose the preaching which demands from them the fulfilling of their major obligations and religious duties.

And this is the point where a person faces the real test of his character and conviction. It is a fact that mere apprehension and recognition of truth is not so difficult, as is adopting it for oneself and inviting others to act upon it and to remaining firm in this struggle. In Quranic terminology, this is called *'istiqamat'* i.e., steadfastness. This is the acid test which proves to what extent a person is committed to his objectives and whether he possesses anything which can be termed stability of character and commitment.

This is why the Holy Quran lays so much emphasis on the fact that true believers necessarily have to face tests and ordeals, and the truthfulness of their claims to have faith is to be examined and tested in many ways. Only those are regarded as sincere in their faith who remain firm in the face of ordeals and provide concrete proof of patience and perseverance.

The Interrelation of Faith, Righteous Deeds and Mutual Exhortation:

We have seen that faith and righteous deeds are interdependent and also exhortation to truth and exhortation to patience. Now, if we understand the relationship between these two pairs, we will have a complete view of this *surah.*

Nothing and no one can avoid influencing his environment and being influenced by it. The coldness of ice will necessarily chill its surroundings and the heat of fire will surely make them warmer. The same is true in the field of morality. If the spirit of righteous deeds is really engendered in a person, it must have an impact upon his environment and he will necessarily be a source of diffusing goodness and virtue. The natural outcome of righteous deeds is the propagation of truth in society.

This principle operates in ethics very forcefully. If the social environment favours evil, it will necessarily bring about deterioration in the lives of its citizens. The only possible way to escape from this is to change that environment or at least to struggle vehemently to change it. Even if a person cannot change it, he can at least in this way, act on the principle that the best defense is a good offence, and repel it defensively. Thus the Holy Prophet (peace be upon him) said:

"If any one among you observes a vice, it is his duty to change it by force, If he is not able to do so, he should protest against it verbally. If he does not possess even this much of courage, he should detest it by his heart and soul, which means that his heart should regard it as bad, and that he should regret that he could not stop it, and this is the weakest degree of faith".

The nobility of a man's character demands exhortation to truth because the goodness in any person who has discovered truth and adopted for himself necessarily demands that he should present it to others, that the greatest number of people may benefit from it, and should partake of its blessing. Thus the Holy Prophet said:

"No one among you can be regarded a believer until he loves for his brother what he loves for himself."

The self-respect and ardent zeal of a man who has accepted truth demand that he should preach it to others. He should uphold it, propagate it, and should sacrifice his life and wealth in the struggle to make it supremely established in society.

If a man adopts a particular way of life and his environment adopts another, then there are only two possibilities. He must either adopt himself to his environment, in that way, removing the discrepancies and resolving clash and discords or, if he finds the environment totally against his wishes, he should put up a tough resistance, should wage war against it, and should try to change it, according to his point of view. Now it is obvious that for a man of dignity, honour, and zeal, a man of earnest concern, the only course open to him is the second one. He would be glad to sacrifice his life for the sake of truth, but would never tolerate that by leading a life of ease and comfort, he should treacherously distort and misrepresent the truth.

Faith, righteous deeds, exhortation to truth and exhortation to patience are indispensable requirements for salvation, and also dependent upon each other. All four are indivisible aspects of a unit, and are inseparable factors of one single totality. In fact, what are all these four except an exposition or commentary of the word faith? If faith has in reality penetrated a person's heart, it will necessarily result in the performance of righteous deeds and if the habit of doing righteous deeds has become one's second nature, its natural outcome would be exhortation to truth; and if the preaching of truth is done with real sincerity and dedication, it will necessarily lead to the stage of exhortation to patience and endurance. The reverse order also holds good. If the stage of preaching patience and endurance is not encountered, then this is a certain proof that the preaching is not of the whole truth, but only of a harmless part of it. If the stage of taking up missionary work is missing, then this implies that a man's actions are not righteous and that he lacks religious zeal. And if his actions are not being performed on the right lines, then this is a categorical proof that genuine faith has not entered his heart.

The path of salvation which is pointed out by *Surah Al-'Asr,* the path of success and triumph towards which it guides and directs us has four mile-stones: faith, righteous deeds, exhortation to truth and exhortation to patience.

The most perfect example of the pattern delineated above is the life-story of the Holy Prophet Muhammad (peace be upon him) wherein all these four components are present in their utmost perfection. At first the Holy Prophet Muhammad (peace be upon him) tried to discover the reality of his own identity and that of the cosmos. A Quranic verse asks:

"And did He not find thee perplexed (and unable to find the right course by thyself) and so He guided (thee)"?

The angel Gabriel revealed to him the truths he required. The Holy Prophet (peace be upon him) confirmed them and affirmed his faith in them, as stated in the Glorious Quran:

"The Messenger believeth in that which hath been revealed unto him from his Lord, and so do the believers."

The life of Prophet Muhammad (saw) was the perfect model of moral excellence and unparalleled example of sublime character. The Holy Quran states: *"And thou standest on an exalted standard of character"*. After fulfilling these fundamental requirements of faith and right- eous deeds to perfection, the Holy Prophet Muhammad (SAW) spent twenty three years in the untiring struggle of preaching the truth and declaring and promulgating the grandeur and glory of Allah. He bravely tolerated all troubles for this purpose, courageously suffered all afflictions and faced all the persecutions and oppressions of his opponents. In the canyon of Bani Hashim, he endured severe hardships during three long years of imprisonment. In the streets of Taif, he was stoned and ridiculed by rascals and urchins. The lives of his dear relatives and his beloved companions were sacrificed for the pleasure of his Lord and in order to uphold divine truth. After indefatigable efforts, struggling night and day for twenty-three years, finally he made the truth reign supreme. And only after making the divine religion *'Islam'* the dominant force in the Arabian peninsula, did he return to his Divine Lord, Allah. May the peace and blessings of Allah be showered on him and on his companions. In short, the biography of the Holy Prophet Muhammad (peace be upon him) embodies the contents of *Surah-Al-'Asr* in action.

So, this is a concise explanation of the significance of *Surah Al-'Asr.* Now you must have realized why I regarded it is the most comprehensive *surah* of the Holy Quran, and why *Imam Al-Shafeii* had said, that if people were to contemplate it seriously, this brief *surah* would be sufficient for their direction and guidance.

Its relation to the surahs before and after:

Finally, let us cast a glance on the surahs of the Holy Quran which precede and follow *Sarah Al- 'Asr.* I had stated that the righteousness of a man's character is based upon the establishment of the real criterion of success and failure in his heart and soul and his willingness to act according to it always. If this criterion is not established, then the aim of his life may be reduced to amassing wealth, material comforts and luxuries. The desire for greater material well-being may overwhelm and over-power his mind to such an extent that it makes him oblivious of the greater realities of his life and the universe. The curtain of this negligence and indifference is only lifted at the time of death. This state of affairs has been described in *Surah 'Al-Takathur* that blessed *surah* of the Glorious Quran which precedes *Surah Al-'Asr.*

As a result of this negligence a man becomes unable to differentiate between right and wrong, lawful and unlawful, approved and forbidden. He sees success as a matter of hoarding and piling up wealth, and he becomes bereft of all good qualities of character and morals, and his personality becomes replete with sins arid vices. This picture has been revealed in *Sarah 'Al-Humaza'* which comes after *Surah Al-'Asr* I seek refuge in Allah, and pray to Him to protect us from such a grievous, dreadful and disastrous end to our lives. Amen!

www.ingramcontent.com/pod-product-compliance
Lightning Source LLC
Chambersburg PA
CBHW062202160726
48282CB00027B/966
9789394834538